Drum-Taps

Walt Whitman

CONTENTS

NOT THE PILOT

YEAR THAT TREMBLED AND REEL'D BENEATH ME

THE WOUND-DRESSER

LONG, TOO LONG AMERICA

GIVE ME THE SPLENDID SILENT SUN

DIRGE FOR TWO VETERANS

OVER THE CARNAGE ROSE PROPHETIC A VOICE

I SAW OLD GENERAL AT BAY

THE ARTILLERYMAN'S VISION

ETHIOPIA SALUTING THE COLOURS

NOT YOUTH PERTAINS TO ME

RACE OF VETERANS

WORLD TAKE GOOD NOTICE

O TAN-FACED PRAIRIE-BOY

LOOK DOWN FAIR MOON

RECONCILIATION

HOW SOLEMN AS ONE BY ONE

AS I LAY WITH MY HEAD IN YOUR LAP CAMERADO

DELICATE CLUSTER

TO A CERTAIN CIVILIAN

LO, VICTRESS ON THE PEAKS

SPIRIT WHOSE WORK IS DONE

ADIEU TO A SOLDIER

TURN O LIBERTAD

TO THE LEAVEN'D SOIL THEY TROD

INTRODUCTION

When the first days of August loured over the world, time seemed to stand still. A universal astonishment and confusion fell, as upon a flock of sheep perplexed by strange dogs. But now, though never before was a St. Lucy's Day so black with "absence, darkness, death, " Christmas is gone. Spring comes swiftly, the almond trees flourish. Easter will soon be here. Life breaks into beauty again and we realize that man may bring hell itself into the world, but that Nature ever patiently waits to be his natural paradise. Yet still a kind of instinctive blindness blots out the prospect of the future. Until the long horror of the war is gone from our minds, we shall be able to think of nothing that has not for its background a chaotic darkness. Like every obsession, it gnaws at thought, follows us into our dreams and returns with the morning. But there have been other wars. And humanity, after learning as best it may their brutal lesson, has survived them. Just as the young soldier leaves home behind him and accepts hardship and danger as to the manner born, so, when he returns again, life will resume its old quiet wont. Nature is not idle even in the imagination. It is man's salvation to forget no less than it is his salvation to remember. And it is wise even in the midst of the conflict to look back on those that are past and to prepare for the returning problems of the future.

When Whitman wrote his "Democratic Vistas, " the long embittered war between the Northern and Southern States of America was a thing only of yesterday. It is a headlong amorphous production—a tangled meadow of "leaves of grass" in prose. But it is as cogent to-day as it was when it was written:

> To the ostent of the senses and eyes [he writes], the influences which stamp the world's history are wars, uprisings, or downfalls of dynasties.... These, of course, play their part; yet, it may be, a single new thought, imagination, abstract principle... put in shape by some great literatus, and projected among mankind, may duly cause changes, growths, removals, greater than the longest and bloodiest war, or the most stupendous merely political, dynastic, or commercial overturn.

The literatus who realized this had his own message in mind. And yet, justly. For those who might point to the worldly prosperity and material comforts of his country, and ask, Are not these better indeed than any utterances even of greatest rhapsodic, artist, or literatus? he has his irrefutable answer. He surveys the New York of 1870, "its façades of marble and iron, of original grandeur and elegance of design, " etc., in his familiar catalogical jargon, and shutting his eyes to its glow and grandeur, inquires in return, Are there indeed *men* here worthy the name? Are there perfect women? Is there a pervading atmosphere of beautiful manners? Are there arts worthy freedom and a rich people? Is there a great moral and religious civilization—the only justification of a great material one? We ourselves in good time shall have to face and to answer these questions. They search our keenest hopes of the peace that is coming. And we may be fortified perhaps by the following queer proof of history repeating itself:

> Never, in the Old World, was thoroughly upholster'd exterior appearance and show, mental and other, built entirely on the idea of caste, and on the sufficiency of mere outside acquisition—never were glibness, verbal intellect, more the test, the emulation—more loftily elevated as head and sample— than they are on the surface of our Republican States this day. The writers of a time hint the mottoes of its gods. The word of the modern, say these voices, is the word Culture.

Whitman had no very tender regard for the Germany of his time. He fancied that the Germans were like the Chinese, only less graceful and refined and more brutish. But neither had he any particular affection for any relic of Europe. "Never again will we trust the moral sense or abstract friendliness of a single *Government* of the Old World. " He accepted selections from its literature for the new American Adam. But even its greatest poets were not America's, and though he might welcome even Juvenal, it was for use and not for worship. We have to learn, he insists, that the best culture will always be that of the manly and courageous instincts and loving perceptions, and of self-respect. In our children rests every hope and promise, and therefore in their mothers. "Disengage yourselves from parties.... These savage and wolfish parties alarm me.... Hold yourself judge and master over all of them. " Only faith can save us, the faith in ourselves and in our fellow-men which is of the true faith in goodness and in God. The idea of the mass of men, so fresh and free, so loving and so proud, filled this poet with a singular awe. Passionately he pleads for the dignity of the common people. It is the average man of a land that is important. To win the people back to a proud belief and confidence in life, to rapture in this wonderful world, to love and admiration—this was his burning desire. I demand races of orbic bards, he rhapsodizes, sweet democratic despots, to dominate and even destroy. The Future! Vistas! The throes of birth are upon us. Allons, camarado!

He could not despair. "Must I indeed learn to chant the cold dirges of the baffled? " he asks himself in "Drum-Taps. " But wildest shuttlecock of criticism though he is, he has never yet been charged with looking only on the dark side of things. Once, he says, "Once, before the war (alas! I dare not say how many times the mood has come!), I too, was fill'd with doubt and gloom. " His part in it soothed, mellowed, deepened his great nature. He had himself witnessed such misery, cruelty, and abomination as it is best just now, perhaps, not to read about. One fact alone is enough; that over fifty thousand Federal soldiers perished of starvation in Southern prisons. Malarial fever contracted in camps and hospitals had wrecked his health. During 1862-65 he visited, he says, eighty to a hundred thousand sick and wounded soldiers, comprehending all, slighting none. Rebel or compatriot, it made no difference. "I loved the young man, " he cries again and again. Pity and fatherliness were in his face, for his heart was full of them. Mr. Gosse has described "the old Gray" as he saw him in 1884, in his bare, littered sun-drenched room in Camden, shared by kitten and canary:

> He sat with a very curious pose of the head thrown backward, as if resting it one vertebra lower down the spinal column than other people do, and thus tilting his face a little upwards. With his head so poised and the whole man fixed in contemplation of the interlocutor he seemed to pass into a state of absolute passivity... the glassy eyes half closed, the large knotted hands spread out before him. He resembled, in fact, nothing so much as "a great old grey Angora Tom, " alert in repose, serenely blinking under his combed waves of hair, with eyes inscrutably dreaming.... As I stood in dull, deserted Mickle Street once more, my heart was full of affection for this beautiful old man... this old rhapsodist in his empty room, glorified by patience and philosophy.

Whitman was then sixty-five. In a portrait of thirty years before there is just a wraith of that feline dream, perhaps, but it is a face of a rare grace and beauty that looks out at us, of a profound kindness and compassion. And, in the eyes, not so much penetration as visionary absorption. Such was the man to whom nothing was unclean, nothing too trivial (except "pale poetlings lisping cadenzas *piano*," who then apparently thronged New York) to take to himself. Intensest, indomitablest of individualists, he exulted in all that appertains to that forked radish, Man. This contentious soul of mine, he exclaims ecstatically; Viva: the attack! I have been born the same as the war was born; I lull nobody, and you will never understand me: maybe I am non-literary and un-decorous.... I have written impromptu, and shall let it all go at that. Let me at least be human! Human, indeed, he was, a tender, all-welcoming host of Everyman, of his idolized (if somewhat overpowering) American democracy. Man in the street, in his swarms, poor crazed faces in the State asylum, prisoners in Sing Sing, prostitute, whose dead body reminded him not of a lost soul, but only of a sad, forlorn, and empty house—it mattered not; he opened his heart to them, one and all. "I see beyond each mark that wonder, a kindred soul. O the bullet could never kill what you really are, dear friend. "

The moon gives you light,
And the bugles and drums give you music,
And my heart, O my soldiers, my veterans,
My heart gives you love.

"Yours for you, " he exclaims, welding in a phrase his unparalleled egotism, his beautiful charity, "yours for you, who ever you are, as mine for me. " It is the essence of philosophy and of religion, for all the wonders of heaven and earth are significant "only because of the Me in the centre. "

This was the secret of his tender, unassuming ministrations. He had none of that shrinking timidity, that fear of intrusion, that uneasiness in the presence of the tragic and the pitiful, which so often numb and oppress those who would willingly give themselves and their best to the needy and suffering, but whose intellect misgives them. He was that formidable phenomenon, a dreamer of action. But he possessed a sovran good sense. Food and rest and clean clothes were his scrupulous preparation for his visits. He always assumed as cheerful an appearance as possible. Armed with bright new five-cent and ten-cent bills (the wounded, he found, were often "broke, " and the sight of a little money "helped their spirits"), with books and stationery and tobacco, for one a twist of good strong green tea, for another a good home-made rice-pudding, or a jar of sparkling but innocent blackberry and cherry syrup, a small bottle of horse-radish pickle, or a large handsome apple, he would "make friends. " "What I have I also give you, " he cried from the bottom of his grieved, tempestuous heart. He would talk, or write letters—passionate love-letters, too—or sit silent, in mute and tender kindness. "Long, long, I gazed... leaning my chin in my hands, passing sweet hours, immortal and mystic hours, with you, dearest comrade—not a tear, not a word, Vigil of silence, love and death, vigil for you my son and my soldier." And how many a mother must have blessed the stranger who could bring such last news of a son as this: "And now like many other noble and good men, after serving his country as a soldier, he has yielded up his young life at the very outset in her service. Such things are gloomy—yet there is a text, 'God doeth all things well'—the meaning of which, after due time, appears to the soul. " It is only love that can comfort the loving.

He forced nothing on these friends of a day, so many of them near their last farewell. A poor wasted young man asks him to read a chapter in the New Testament, and Whitman chooses that which describes Christ's Crucifixion. He "ask'd me to read the following chapter also, how Christ rose again. I read very slowly, for he was feeble. It pleased him very much, yet the tears were in his eyes. He ask'd me if I enjoy'd religion. I said 'Perhaps not, my dear, in the way you mean, yet maybe, it is the same thing. '" This is only one of many such serene intimacies in Whitman's experiences of the war. Through them we reach to an understanding of a poet who chose not signal and beautiful episodes out of the past, nor the rare moments of existence, for theme, but took all life, within and around him in vast bustling America, for his poetic province. Like a benign barbaric sun he surveys the world, ever at noon. I am the man, I suffer'd, I was there, he cries in the "Song of Myself. " I do not despise you priests, all times, the world over.... He could not despise anything, not even his fellow-poets, because he himself was everything. His verse sometimes seems mere verbiage, but it is always a higgledy-piggledy, Santa Claus bagful of *things*. And he could penetrate to the essential reality. He tells in his "Drum-Taps" how one daybreak he arose in camp, and saw three still forms stretched out in the eastern radiance, how with light fingers he just lifted the blanket from each cold face in turn: the first elderly, gaunt, and grim—Who are you, my dear comrade? The next with cheeks yet blooming—Who are you, sweet boy? The third—Young man, I think I know you. I think this face is the face of the Christ Himself, Dead and divine and brother of all, and here again he lies.

True poetry focuses experience, not merely transmits it. It must redeem it for ever from transitoriness and evanescence. Whitman incontinently pours experience out in a Niagara-like cataract. But in spite of his habitual publicity he was at heart of a "shy, brooding, impassioned devotional type"; in spite of his self-conscious, arrogant virility, he was to the end of his life an entranced child. He came into the world, saw and babbled. His deliberate method of writing could have had no other issue. A subject would occur to him, a kind of tag. He would scribble it down on a scrap of paper and drop it into a drawer. Day by day this first impulse would evoke fresh "poemets, " until at length the accumulation was exhaustive. Then he merely gutted his treasury and the ode was complete. It was only when sense and feeling attained a sort of ecstasy that he succeeded in distilling the true essence that is poetry and in enstopping it in a crystal phial of form.

The prose of his "Specimen Days, " indeed, is often nearer to poetry than his verse:

> Much of the time he sleeps, or half sleeps.... I often come and sit by him in perfect silence; he will breathe for ten minutes as softly and evenly as a young babe asleep. Poor youth, so handsome, athletic, with profuse beautiful shining hair. One time as I sat looking at him while he lay asleep, he suddenly, without the least start awaken'd, open'd his eyes, gave me a long steady look, turning his face very slightly to gaze easier—one long, clear, silent look—a slight sigh—then turn'd back and went into his doze again. Little he knew, poor death-stricken boy, the heart of the stranger that hover'd near.

> The western star, Venus, in the earlier hours of evening has never been so large, so clear; it seems as if it told something, as if it held rapport indulgent with humanity, with us Americans. The sky dark blue, the transparent night, the planets, the moderate west wind, the elastic temperature, the miracle of that great star, and the young and swelling moon swimming in the west, suffused the soul. Then I heard slow and clear the deliberate notes of a bugle come up out of the

silence... firm and faithful, floating along, rising, falling leisurely, with here and there a long-drawn note.... sounding tattoo.

"A steady rain, dark and thick and warm, " he writes again, two days after Gettysburg. "The cavalry camp is a ceaseless field of observation to me. This forenoon there stood the horses, tether'd together, dripping, steaming, chewing their hay. The men emerge from their tents, dripping also. The fires are half-quench'd. " There is a poetic poise in this brief, vivid statement, apart from its bare economy of means. It is the lump awaiting the leaven no less than is "Cavalry Crossing a Ford. " To this supreme spectator an apple orchard in May, even the White House in moonlight, no more and no less than these battle-scenes, rendered up their dignity, life, and beauty, their true human significance. But in "Drum-Taps" the witness is not always so satisfactory. The secret has evaporated in the effort to *make* poetry, or half-consciously to inject a moral, to play the Universal Bard. There creeps into the words a tinge of the raw and the grotesque. The poet has the look of a cowboy off the stage, tanned with grease-paint. But again and again the secret creeps back and some lovely emanation of poetry is added to it:

Look down fair moon and bathe this scene,
Pour softly down night's nimbus floods on faces ghastly,
    swollen, purple,
On the dead on their backs with arms toss'd wide, Pour
down your unstinted nimbus sacred moon.

Or this, called "Reconciliation":

Word over all, beautiful as the sky,
Beautiful that war and all its deeds of carnage must in time be
    utterly lost,
That the hands of the sisters Death and Night incessantly
    softly wash again, and ever again, this soil'd world;
For my enemy is dead, a man divine as myself is dead, I
look where he lies white-faced and still in the coffin—I draw
    near,
Bend down and touch lightly with my lips the white face in the
    coffin.

The bonds of rhyme shackled him, deprived him of more than freedom. He is like a wild bird that suddenly perceives the bars of its small cage across the blue of the sky. And yet the finer his poems are, the nearer they approach to definite rhythmical design. One has only to compare "O Captain! my Captain! " with "Hushed be the Camps To-day" to perceive this curious paradox. They are both of them memories of his beloved Lincoln, whom he had many times seen, with that peculiarly close and transatlantic curiosity of his, riding at a jog-trot, on a good-sized, easy-going grey horse, with his escort of yellow-striped cavalry behind him, through the streets of Washington—dressed in black, somewhat rusty and dusty, with a black, stiff hat, almost as ordinary in attire as the commonest man. That heroic face, too, he had pierced; and caught from it the deep, subtle, indirect expression, that only the long-gone master-painters of the Old World could have seized and immortalized. And in yet another memory of this great American Whitman attains to his best and highest, "When Lilacs Last in the Doorway Bloom'd. " It is one of the most beautiful of poems, of the purest intuition, of a consummate, if unconscious, artistry. Whose voice is it that rings and echoes, now low and tender, now solemn and desolate, now clear, full, victorious, out of its cloistral solitude—that of the mourner himself, of all-heedfull, heedless Nature, of the immortal soul of man, or just a bird, the shy and hidden, sweet, small hermit thrush? The last division of his life's work—his fond Epic, his cosmic "inventory"—as Whitman planned it, was to be devoted to the chaunting of songs of death and immortality. The soldier to whom he read of Christ's Resurrection talked of death to him, and said he did not fear it. He talked to a man who did not enjoy religion in the way a Christian means, to whom the mystery of Easter is an all-sufficing "reliance. " But Whitman not only did not fear death. The thought of it was to him the strangest of raptures, the reverie of a child dreaming of a distant mother, soon to come again. Death and immortality were but two aspects of the same blessed hope to this man, who poured out his life in a turgid fount of ecstatic joy in living:

... And I saw askant the armies,
 I saw as in noiseless dreams hundreds of battle-flags,
 Borne through the smoke of the battles and pierc'd with missiles I
      saw them,
 And carried hither and yon through the smoke, and torn and bloody,
 And at last but a few shreds left on the staffs (and all in silence),
 And the staffs all splintered and broken.

I saw battle-corpses, myriads of them,
And the white skeletons of young men, I saw them,
I saw the debris and debris of all the slain soldiers of the war,
But I saw they were not as was thought,
They themselves were fully at rest, they suffer'd not,
The living remain'd and suffer'd, the mother suffer'd,
And the wives and the child and the musing comrade suffer'd,
And the armies that remain'd suffer'd....

Come lovely and soothing death,
Undulate round the world, serenely arriving, arriving,
In the night, in the day, to all, to each,
Sooner or later delicate death.

Prais'd be the fathomless universe,
For life and joy, and for objects and knowledge curious,
And for love, sweet love—but praise! praise! praise!
For the sure-enwinding arms of cool-enfolding death.

Dark mother always gliding near with soft feet
Have none chanted for thee a chant of fullest welcome?
Then I chant it for thee, I glorify thee above all,
I bring thee a song that when thou must indeed come, come
    unfalteringly.

FIRST O SONGS FOR A PRELUDE.

First O songs for a prelude,
Lightly strike on the stretch'd tympanum pride and joy in my city,
How she led the rest to arms, how she gave the cue,
How at once with lithe limbs unwaiting a moment she sprang,
(O superb! O Manhattan, my own, my peerless!
O strongest you in the hour of danger, in crisis! O truer than steel!)
How you sprang—how you threw off the costumes of peace with
        indifferent hand,
How your soft opera-music changed, and the drum and fife were
        heard in their stead,
How you led to the war, (that shall serve for our prelude, songs of
        soldiers,)
How Manhattan drum-taps led.

Forty years had I in my city seen soldiers parading,
Forty years as a pageant, still unawares the lady of this teeming and
        turbulent city,
Sleepless amid her ships, her houses, her incalculable wealth,
With her million children around her, suddenly,
At dead of night, at news from the south,
Incens'd struck with clinch'd hand the pavement.

A shock electric, the night sustain'd it,
Till with ominous hum our hive at daybreak pour'd out its myriads.
From the houses then and the workshops, and through all the doorways,
Leapt they tumultuous, and lo! Manhattan arming.

To the drum-taps prompt,
The young men falling in and arming,
The mechanics arming, (the trowel, the jack-plane, the blacksmith's
        hammer, tost aside with precipitation,)
The lawyer leaving his office and arming, the judge leaving the court,
The driver deserting his wagon in the street, jumping down, throwing
        the reins abruptly down on the horses' backs,
The salesman leaving the store, the boss, book-keeper, porter, all leaving;
  Squads gather everywhere by common consent and arm,
  The new recruits, even boys, the old men show them how to wear their
       accoutrements, they buckle the straps carefully,

Outdoors arming, indoors arming, the flash of the musketbarrels,
The white tents cluster in camps, the arm'd sentries around, the
      sunrise cannon and again at sunset,
Arm'd regiments arrive every day, pass through the city, and embark
      from the wharves,
(How good they look as they tramp down to the river, sweaty, with
      their guns on their shoulders!
How I love them! how I could hug them, with their brown faces and
      their clothes and knapsacks cover'd with dust!)
The blood of the city up—arm'd! arm'd! the cry everywhere,
The flags flung out from the steeples of churches and from all the
      public buildings and stores,
The tearful parting, the mother kisses her son, the son kisses his
      mother,
(Loth is the mother to part, yet not a word does she speak to detain
      him,)
The tumultuous escort, the ranks of policemen preceding, clearing the
      way,
The unpent enthusiasm, the wild cheers of the crowd for the
      favorites,
The artillery, the silent cannons bright as gold, drawn along, rumble
      lightly over the stones,
(Silent cannons, soon to cease your silence,
Soon unlimber'd to begin the red business;)
All the mutter of preparation, all the determin'd arming,
The hospital service, the lint, bandages and medicines,
The women volunteering for nurses, the work begun for in earnest, no
      mere parade now;
War! an arm'd race is advancing! the welcome for battle, no turning
      away;
War! be it weeks, months, or years, an arm'd race is advancing to
      welcome it.

Mannahatta a-march—and it's O to sing it well!
It's O for a manly life in the camp.

And the sturdy artillery,
The guns bright as gold, the work for giants, to serve well the guns,
Unlimber them! (no more as the past forty years for salutes for
      courtesies merely,
Put in something now besides powder and wadding.)

And you lady of ships, you Mannahatta,

Drum-Taps

Old matron of this proud, friendly, turbulent city,
Often in peace and wealth you were pensive or covertly frown'd amid
    all your children,
But now you smile with joy exulting old Mannahatta.

EIGHTEEN SIXTY-ONE.

Arm'd year—year of the struggle,
 No dainty rhymes or sentimental love verses for you terrible year,
 Not you as some pale poetling seated at a desk lisping cadenzas
      piano,
 But as a strong man erect, clothed in blue clothes, advancing,
      carrying a rifle on your shoulder,
 With well-gristled body and sunburnt face and hands, with a knife in
      the belt at your side,
 As I heard you shouting loud, your sonorous voice ringing across the
      continent,
 Your masculine voice O year, as rising amid the great cities,
 Amid the men of Manhattan I saw you as one of the workmen, the
      dwellers in Manhattan,
 Or with large steps crossing the prairies out of Illinois and Indiana,
 Rapidly crossing the West with springy gait and descending the
      Alleghanies,
 Or down from the great lakes or in Pennsylvania, or on deck along the
      Ohio river,
 Or southward along the Tennessee or Cumberland rivers, or at
      Chattanooga on the mountain top,
 Saw I your gait and saw I your sinewy limbs clothed in blue, bearing
      weapons, robust year,
 Heard your determin'd voice launch'd forth again and again,
 Year that suddenly sang by the mouths of the round-lipp'd cannon,
 I repeat you, hurrying, crashing, sad, distracted year.

BEAT! BEAT! DRUMS!

Beat! beat! drums!—blow! bugles! blow!
  Through the windows-through doors-burst like a ruthless force,
  Into the solemn church, and scatter the congregation,
  Into the school where the scholar is studying;
  Leave not the bridegroom quiet—no happiness must he have now with
        his bride,
  Nor the peaceful farmer any peace, ploughing his field or gathering
        his grain,
  So fierce you whirr and pound you drums—so shrill you bugles blow.

Beat! beat! drums!—blow! bugles! blow!
  Over the traffic of cities—over the rumble of wheels in the streets;
  Are beds prepared for sleepers at night in the houses? no sleepers
        must sleep in those beds,
  No bargainers' bargains by day—no brokers or speculators—would they
        continue?
  Would the talkers be talking? would the singer attempt to sing?
  Would the lawyer rise in the court to state his case before the
        judge?
  Then rattle quicker, heavier drums—you bugles wilder blow.

Beat! beat! drums!—blow! bugles! blow!
  Make no parley—stop for no expostulation,
  Mind not the timid—mind not the weeper or prayer,
  Mind not the old man beseeching the young man,
  Let not the child's voice be heard, nor the mother's entreaties,
  Make even the trestles to shake the dead where they lie awaiting the
        hearses,
  So strong you thump O terrible drums—so loud you bugles blow.

FROM PAUMANOK STARTING I FLY LIKE A BIRD

From Paumanok starting I fly like a bird,
  Around and around to soar to sing the idea of all,
  To the north betaking myself to sing there arctic songs,
  To Kanada till I absorb Kanada in myself, to Michigan then,
  To Wisconsin, Iowa, Minnesota, to sing their songs, (they are
          inimitable;)
  Then to Ohio and Indiana to sing theirs, to Missouri and Kansas and
          Arkansas to sing theirs,
  To Tennessee and Kentucky, to the Carolinas and Georgia to sing
          theirs,
  To Texas and so along up toward California, to roam accepted
          everywhere;
  To sing first, (to the tap of the war-drum if need be,)
  The idea of all, of the Western world one and inseparable,
          And then the song of each member of these States.

SONG OF THE BANNER AT DAYBREAK.

Poet.
O a new song, a free song,
Flapping, flapping, flapping, flapping, by sounds, by voices clearer,
By the wind's voice and that of the drum,
By the banner's voice and child's voice and sea's voice and father's
     voice,
Low on the ground and high in the air,
On the ground where father and child stand,
In the upward air where their eyes turn,
Where the banner at daybreak is flapping.

Words! bookwords! what are you?
Words no more, for hearken and see,
My song is there in the open air, and I must sing,
With the banner and pennant a-flapping.

I'll weave the chord and twine in,
Man's desire and babe's desire, I'll twine them in, I'll put in life,
I'll put the bayonet's flashing point, I'll let bullets and slugs whizz,
(As one carrying a symbol and menace far into the future,
Crying with trumpet voice, *Arouse and beware! Beware and arouse!*)
I'll pour the verse with streams of blood, full of volition, full of joy.
Then loosen, launch forth, to go and compete,
With the banner and pennant a-flapping.

Pennant.
Come up here, bard, bard,
Come up here, soul, soul,
Come up here, dear little child,
To fly in the clouds and winds with me, and play with the measureless
     light.

Child.
Father what is that in the sky beckoning to me with long finger?
And what does it say to me all the while?

Father.
Nothing my babe you see in the sky,
And nothing at all to you it says—but look you my babe,

Look at these dazzling things in the houses, and see you the
    money-shops opening,
And see you the vehicles preparing to crawl along the streets with
    goods;
These, ah these, how valued and toil'd for these!
How envied by all the earth.

Poet.
Fresh and rosy red the sun is mounting high,
On floats the sea in distant blue careering through its channels,
On floats the wind over the breast of the sea setting in toward land,
The great steady wind from west or west-by-south,
Floating so buoyant with milk-white foam on the waters.

But I am not the sea nor the red sun,
I am not the wind with girlish laughter,
Not the immense wind which strengthens, not the wind which lashes,
Not the spirit that ever lashes its own body to terror and death,
But I am that which unseen comes and sings, sings, sings,
Which babbles in brooks and scoots in showers on the land,
Which the birds know in the woods mornings and evenings,
And the shore-sands know and the hissing wave, and that banner and
    pennant,
Aloft there flapping and flapping.

Child.
O father it is alive—it is full of people—it has children,
O now it seems to me it is talking to its children,
I hear it—it talks to me—O it is wonderful!
O it stretches—it spreads and runs so fast—O my father,
It is so broad it covers the whole sky.

Father.
Cease, cease, my foolish babe,
What you are saying is sorrowful to me, much it displeases me;
Behold with the rest again I say, behold not banners and pennants
    aloft,
But the well-prepared pavements behold, and mark the solid-wall'd
    houses.

Banner and Pennant.
Speak to the child O bard out of Manhattan,
To our children all, or north or south of Manhattan,

Point this day, leaving all the rest, to us over all—and yet we know
    not why,
For what are we, mere strips of cloth profiting nothing,
Only flapping in the wind?

Poet.
I hear and see not strips of cloth alone,
I hear the tramp of armies, I hear the challenging sentry,
I hear the jubilant shouts of millions of men, I hear Liberty!
I hear the drums beat and the trumpets blowing,
I myself move abroad swift-rising flying then,
I use the wings of the land-bird and use the wings of the sea-bird,
    and look down as from a height,
I do not deny the precious results of peace, I see populous cities
    with wealth incalculable,
I see numberless farms, I see the farmers working in their fields or
    barns,
I see mechanics working, I see buildings everywhere founded, going
    up, or finished,
I see trains of cars swiftly speeding along railroad tracks drawn by
    the locomotives,
I see the stores, depots, of Boston, Baltimore, Charleston, New
    Orleans,
I see far in the West the immense area of grain, I dwell awhile
    hovering,
I pass to the lumber forests of the North, and again to the Southern
    plantation, and again to California;
Sweeping the whole I see the countless profit, the busy gatherings,
    earn'd wages,
See the Identity formed out of thirty-eight spacious and haughty
    States, (and many more to come,)
See forts on the shores of harbors, see ships sailing in and out;
Then over all, (aye! aye!) my little and lengthen'd pennant shaped
    like a sword,
Runs swiftly up indicating war and defiance—and now the halyards
    have rais'd it,
Side of my banner broad and blue, side of my starry banner,
Discarding peace over all the sea and land.

Banner and Pennant.
Yet louder, higher, stronger, bard! yet farther, wider cleave!
No longer let our children deem us riches and peace alone,
We may be terror and carnage, and are so now,

Not now are we any one of these spacious and haughty States, (nor any
　　five, nor ten,)
Nor market nor depot we, nor money-bank in the city,
But these and all, and the brown and spreading land, and the mines
　　below, are ours,
And the shores of the sea are ours, and the rivers great and small,
And the fields they moisten, and the crops and the fruits are ours,
Bays and channels and ships sailing in and out are ours—while we
　　over all,
Over the area spread below, the three or four millions of square
　　miles, the capitals,
The forty millions of people,—O bard! in life and death supreme,
We, even we, henceforth flaunt out masterful, high up above,
Not for the present alone, for a thousand years chanting through you,
This song to the soul of one poor little child.

Child.
O my father I like not the houses,
They will never to me be any thing, nor do I like money,
But to mount up there I would like, O father dear, that banner I
　　like,
That pennant I would be and must be.

Father.
Child of mine you fill me with anguish,
To be that pennant would be too fearful,
Little you know what it is this day, and after this day, forever,
It is to gain nothing, but risk and defy every thing,
Forward to stand in front of wars—and O, such wars!—what have you
　　to do with them?
With passions of demons, slaughter, premature death?

Banner.
Demons and death then I sing,
Put in all, aye all will I, sword-shaped pennant for war,
And a pleasure new and ecstatic, and the prattled yearning of
　　children,
Blent with the sounds of the peaceful land and the liquid wash of the
　　sea,
And the black ships fighting on the sea envelop'd in smoke,
And the icy cool of the far, far north, with rustling cedars and
　　pines,
And the whirr of drums and the sound of soldiers marching, and the

hot sun shining south,
And the beach-waves combing over the beach on my Eastern shore, and
    my Western shore the same,
And all between those shores, and my ever running Mississippi with
    bends and chutes,
And my Illinois fields, and my Kansas fields, and my fields of
    Missouri,
The Continent, devoting the whole identity without reserving an atom,
Pour in! whelm that which asks, which sings, with all and the yield
    of all,
Fusing and holding, claiming, devouring the whole,
No more with tender lip, nor musical labial sound,
But out of the night emerging for good, our voice persuasive no more,
Croaking like crows here in the wind.

Poet.
My limbs, my veins dilate, my theme is clear at last,
Banner so broad advancing out of the night, I sing you haughty and
    resolute,
I burst through where I waited long, too long, deafen'd and blinded,
My hearing and tongue are come to me, (a little child taught me,)
I hear from above O pennant of war your ironical call and demand,
Insensate! insensate! (yet I at any rate chant you,) O banner!
Not houses of peace indeed are you, nor any nor all their prosperity,
    (if need be, you shall again have every one of those houses
    to destroy them,
You thought not to destroy those valuable houses, standing fast, full
    of comfort, built with money,
May they stand fast, then? not an hour except you above them and all
    stand fast;)
O banner, not money so precious are you, not farm produce you, nor
    the material good nutriment,
Nor excellent stores, nor landed on wharves from the ships,
Not the superb ships with sail-power or steam-power, fetching and
    carrying cargoes,
Nor machinery, vehicles, trade, nor revenues—but you as henceforth I
    see you,
Running up out of the night, bringing your cluster of stars,
    (ever-enlarging stars,)
Divider of daybreak you, cutting the air, touch'd by the sun,
    measuring the sky,
(Passionately seen and yearn'd for by one poor little child,
While others remain busy or smartly talking, forever teaching thrift,

thrift;)

O you up there! O pennant! where you undulate like a snake hissing so
    curious,

Out of reach, an idea only, yet furiously fought for, risking bloody
    death, loved by me,

So loved—O you banner leading the day with stars brought from the
    night!

Valueless, object of eyes, over all and demanding all—(absolute
    owner of all)—O banner and pennant!

I too leave the rest—great as it is, it is nothing—houses, machines
    are nothing—I see them not,

I see but you, O warlike pennant! O banner so broad, with stripes, I
    sing you only,

Flapping up there in the wind.

RISE O DAYS FROM YOUR FATHOMLESS DEEPS.

1

Rise O days from your fathomless deeps, till you loftier, fiercer
  sweep,
Long for my soul hungering gymnastic I devour'd what the earth gave
  me,
Long I roam'd the woods of the north, long I watch'd Niagara pouring,
I travel'd the prairies over and slept on their breast, I cross'd the
  Nevadas, I cross'd the plateaus,
I ascended the towering rocks along the Pacific, I sail'd out to sea,
I sail'd through the storm, I was refresh'd by the storm,
I watch'd with joy the threatening maws of the waves,
I mark'd the white combs where they career'd so high, curling over,
I heard the wind piping, I saw the black clouds,
Saw from below what arose and mounted (O superb! O wild as my heart,
  and powerful!)
Heard the continuous thunder as it bellow'd after the lightning,
Noted the slender and jagged threads of lightning as sudden and fast
  amid the din they chased each other across the sky;
These, and such as these, I, elate, saw—saw with wonder, yet pensive
  and masterful,
All the menacing might of the globe uprisen around me,
Yet there with my soul I fed, I fed content, supercilious.

2

'Twas well, O soul—'twas a good preparation you gave me,
Now we advance our latent and ampler hunger to fill,
Now we go forth to receive what the earth and the sea never gave us,
Not through the mighty woods we go, but through the mightier cities,
Something for us is pouring now more than Niagara pouring,
Torrents of men, (sources and rills of the Northwest are you indeed
  inexhaustible?)
What, to pavements and homesteads here, what were those storms of the
  mountains and sea?
What, to passions I witness around me to-day? was the sea risen?
Was the wind piping the pipe of death under the black clouds?
Lo! from deeps more unfathomable, something more deadly and savage,

Manhattan rising, advancing with menacing front—Cincinnati,
　　　　Chicago, unchain'd;
What was that swell I saw on the ocean? behold what comes here,
How it climbs with daring feet and hands—how it dashes!
How the true thunder bellows after the lightning—how bright the
　　　　flashes of lightning!
How Democracy with desperate vengeful port strides on, shown
　　　　through the dark by those flashes of lightning!
(Yet a mournful wail and low sob I fancied I heard through the dark,
In a lull of the deafening confusion.)

3

Thunder on! stride on, Democracy! strike with vengeful stroke!
And do you rise higher than ever yet O days, O cities!
Crash heavier, heavier yet O storms! you have done me good,
My soul prepared in the mountains absorbs your immortal strong
　　　　nutriment,
Long had I walk'd my cities, my country roads through farms, only
　　　　half satisfied,
One doubt nauseous undulating like a snake, crawl'd on the ground
　　　　before me,
Continually preceding my steps, turning upon me oft, ironically
　　　　hissing low;
The cities I loved so well I abandon'd and left, I sped to the
　　　　certainties suitable to me,
Hungering, hungering, hungering, for primal energies and Nature's
　　　　dauntlessness,
I refresh'd myself with it only, I could relish it only,
I waited the bursting forth of the pent fire—on the water and air I
　　　　waited long;
But now I no longer wait, I am fully satisfied, I am glutted,
I have witness'd the true lightning, I have witness'd my cities
　　　　electric,
I have lived to behold man burst forth and warlike America rise,
Hence I will seek no more the food of the northern solitary wilds,
　　　　No more the mountains roam or sail the stormy sea.

VIRGINIA—THE WEST.

The noble sire fallen on evil days,
  I saw with hand uplifted, menacing, brandishing,
  (Memories of old in abeyance, love and faith in abeyance,)
  The insane knife toward the Mother of All.

The noble son on sinewy feet advancing,
  I saw, out of the land of prairies, land of Ohio's waters and of
      Indiana,
  To the rescue the stalwart giant hurry his plenteous offspring,
  Drest in blue, bearing their trusty rifles on their shoulders.

Then the Mother of All with calm voice speaking,
  As to you Rebellious, (I seemed to hear her say,) why strive against
      me, and why seek my life?
  When you yourself forever provide to defend me?
  For you provided me Washington—and now these also.

CITY OF SHIPS.

City of ships!
(O the black ships! O the fierce ships!
O the beautiful sharp-bow'd steam-ships and sail-ships!)
City of the world! (for all races are here,
All the lands of the earth make contributions here;)
City of the sea! city of hurried and glittering tides!
City whose gleeful tides continually rush or recede, whirling in and
        out with eddies and foam!
City of wharves and stores—city of tall façades of marble and iron!
Proud and passionate city—mettlesome, mad, extravagant city!
Spring up, O city—not for peace alone, but be indeed yourself,
        warlike!
Fear not—submit to no models but your own O city!
Behold me—incarnate me as I have incarnated you!
I have rejected nothing you offer'd me—whom you adopted I have
        adopted,
Good or bad I never question you—I love all—I do not condemn
        anything,
I chant and celebrate all that is yours—yet peace no more,
In peace I chanted peace, but now the drum of war is mine,
War, red war is my song through your streets, O city!

THE CENTENARIAN'S STORY.

Volunteer of 1861-2, (at Washington Park, Brooklyn, assisting the Centenarian.)

Give me your hand old Revolutionary,
  The hill-top is nigh, but a few steps, (make room gentlemen,)
  Up the path you have follow'd me well, spite of your hundred and
      extra years,
  You can walk old man, though your eyes are almost done,
  Your faculties serve you, and presently I must have them serve me.
  Rest, while I tell what the crowd around us means,
  On the plain below recruits are drilling and exercising,
  There is the camp, one regiment departs to-morrow,
  Do you hear the officers giving their orders?
  Do you hear the clank of the muskets?

Why what comes over you now old man?
  Why do you tremble and clutch my hand so convulsively?
  The troops are but drilling, they are yet surrounded with smiles.
  Around them at hand the well-drest friends and the women,
  While splendid and warm the afternoon sun shines down,
  Green the midsummer verdure and fresh blows the dallying breeze,
  O'er proud and peaceful cities and arm of the sea between.
  But drill and parade are over, they march back to quarters,
  Only hear that approval of hands! hear what a clapping!

As wending the crowds now part and disperse—but we old man,
  Not for nothing have I brought you hither—we must remain,
  You to speak in your turn, and I to listen and tell.

The Centenarian.

When I clutch'd your hand it was not with terror,
  But suddenly pouring about me here on every side,
  And below there where the boys were drilling, and up the slopes they
      ran,
  And where tents are pitch'd, and wherever you see south and
      south-east and south-west,
  Over hills, across lowlands, and in the skirts of woods,
  And along the shores, in mire (now fill'd over) came again and

suddenly raged,
As eighty-five years a-gone no mere parade receiv'd with applause of
    friends,
But a battle which I took part in myself—aye, long ago as it is I
    took part in it,
Walking then this hill-top, this same ground.

Aye, this is the ground,
My blind eyes even as I speak behold it re-peopled from graves,
The years recede, pavements and stately houses disappear,
Rude forts appear again, the old hoop'd guns are mounted,
I see the lines of rais'd earth stretching from river to bay,
I mark the vista of waters, I mark the uplands and slopes;
Here we lay encamp'd, it was this time in summer also.

As I talk I remember all, I remember the Declaration,
It was read here, the whole army paraded, it was read to us here,
By his staff surrounded the General stood in the middle, he held up
    his unsheath'd sword,
It glitter'd in the sun in full sight of the army.

'Twas a bold act then—the English war-ships had just arrived,
We could watch down the lower bay where they lay at anchor,
And the transports swarming with soldiers.

A few days more and they landed, and then the battle.

Twenty thousand were brought against us,
A veteran force furnish'd with good artillery.
I tell not now the whole of the battle,
But one brigade early in the forenoon order'd forward to engage the
    red-coats,
Of that brigade I tell, and how steadily it march'd,
And how long and well it stood confronting death.

Who do you think that was marching steadily sternly confronting
    death?
It was the brigade of the youngest men, two thousand strong,
Raised in Virginia and Maryland, and most of them known
personally to the General.

Jauntily forward they went with quick step toward Gowanus' waters,
Till of a sudden unlook'd for by defiles through the woods, gain'd at

night,
The British advancing, rounding in from the east, fiercely playing
    their guns,
That brigade of the youngest was cut off and at the enemy's mercy.

The General watch'd them from this hill,
They made repeated desperate attempts to burst their environment,
They drew close together, very compact, their flag flying in the
    middle,
But O from the hills how the cannon were thinning and thinning them!

It sickens me yet, that slaughter!
I saw the moisture gather in drops on the face of the General.
I saw how he wrung his hands in anguish.

Meanwhile the British manoeuvr'd to draw us out for a pitch'd battle,
But we dared not trust the chances of a pitch'd battle.

We fought the fight in detachments.
Sallying forth we fought at several points, but in each the luck was
    against us,
Our foe advancing, steadily getting the best of it, push'd us back to
    the works on this hill,
Till we turn'd menacing here, and then he left us.

That was the going out of the brigade of the youngest men, two
    thousand strong,
Few return'd, nearly all remain in Brooklyn.
That and here my General's first battle,
No women looking on nor sunshine to bask in, it did not conclude with
    applause,
Nobody clapp'd hands here then.

But in darkness in mist on the ground under a chill rain,
Wearied that night we lay foil'd and sullen,
While scornfully laugh'd many an arrogant lord oft' against us
    encamp'd,
Quite within hearing, feasting, clinking wineglasses together over
    their victory.

So dull and damp and another day,
But the night of that, mist lifting, rain ceasing,
Silent as a ghost while they thought they were sure of him, my

General retreated.

I saw him at the river-side,
Down by the ferry lit by torches, hastening the embarcation;
My General waited till the soldiers and wounded were all pass'd over,
And then, (it was just ere sunrise,) these eyes rested on him for the
    last time.

Every one else seem'd fill'd with gloom,
Many no doubt thought of capitulation.

But when my General pass'd me,
As he stood in his boat and look'd toward the coming sun,
I saw something different from capitulation.

Terminus.

Enough, the Centenarian's story ends,
The two, the past and present, have interchanged,
I myself as connecter, as chansonnier of a great future, am now
    speaking.

And is this the ground Washington trod?
And these waters I listlessly daily cross, are these the waters he
    cross'd,
As resolute in defeat as other generals in their proudest triumphs?

I must copy the story, and send it eastward and westward,
I must preserve that look as it beam'd on you rivers of Brooklyn.

See—as the annual round returns the phantoms return,
It is the 27th of August and the British have landed,
The battle begins and goes against us, behold through the smoke
    Washington's face,
The brigade of Virginia and Maryland have march'd forth to intercept
    the enemy,
They are cut off, murderous artillery from the hills plays upon them,
Rank after rank falls, while over them silently droops the flag,
Baptized that day in many a young man's bloody wounds,
In death, defeat, and sisters', mothers' tears.
Ah, hills and slopes of Brooklyn! I perceive you are more valuable

than your owners supposed;
In the midst of you stands an encampment very old,
Stands forever the camp of that dead brigade.

CAVALRY CROSSING A FORD.

A line in long array where they wind betwixt green islands,
  They take a serpentine course, their arms flash in the sun—hark to
      the musical clank,
  Behold the silvery river, in it the splashing horses loitering stop
      to drink,
  Behold the brown-faced men, each group, each person a picture, the
      negligent rest on the saddles,
  Some emerge on the opposite bank, others are just entering the
      ford—while
  Scarlet and blue and snowy white,
  The guidon flags flutter gayly in the wind.

BIVOUAC ON A MOUNTAIN SIDE.

I see before me now a traveling army halting,
  Below a fertile valley spread, with barns and the orchards of summer,
  Behind, the terraced sides of a mountain, abrupt, in places rising
      high,
  Broken, with rocks, with clinging cedars, with tall shapes dingily
      seen,
  The numerous camp-fires scatter'd near and far, some away up on the
      mountain,
  The shadowy forms of men and horses, looming, large-sized,
      flickering,
  And over all the sky—the sky! far, far out of reach, studded,
      breaking out, the eternal stars.

AN ARMY CORPS ON THE MARCH.

With its cloud of skirmishers in advance,
With now the sound of a single shot snapping like a whip, and now an
      irregular volley,
  The swarming ranks press on and on, the dense brigades press on,
  Glittering dimly, toiling under the sun—the dust-cover'd men,
  In columns rise and fall to the undulations of the ground,
  With artillery interspers'd—the wheels rumble, the horses sweat,
      As the army corps advances.

BY THE BIVOUAC'S FITFUL FLAME.

By the bivouac's fitful flame,
  A procession winding around me, solemn and sweet and slow—but first
      I note,
  The tents of the sleeping army, the fields' and woods' dim out-line,
  The darkness lit by spots of kindled fire, the silence,
  Like a phantom far or near an occasional figure moving,
  The shrubs and trees, (as I lift my eyes they seem to be stealthily
      watching me,)
  While wind in procession thoughts, O tender and wondrous thoughts,
  Of life and death, of home and the past and loved, and of those that
      are far away;
  A solemn and slow procession there as I sit on the ground,
  By the bivouac's fitful flame.

COME UP FROM THE FIELDS FATHER.

Come up from the fields father, here's a letter from our Pete,
  And come to the front door mother, here's a letter from thy dear son.

Lo, 'tis autumn,
Lo, where the trees, deeper green, yellower and redder,
Cool and sweeten Ohio's villages with leaves fluttering in the
      moderate wind,
Where apples ripe in the orchards hang and grapes on the trellis'd
      vines,
(Smell you the smell of the grapes on the vines?
Smell you the buckwheat where the bees were lately buzzing?)
Above all, lo, the sky so calm, so transparent after the rain, and
      with wondrous clouds,
Below too, all calm, all vital and beautiful, and the farm prospers
      well.

Down in the fields all prospers well,
But now from the fields come father, come at the daughter's call,
And come to the entry mother, to the front door come right away.

Fast as she can she hurries, something ominous, her steps trembling,
She does not tarry to smooth her hair nor adjust her cap.

Open the envelope quickly,
O this is not our son's writing, yet his name is sign'd,
O a strange hand writes for our dear son, O stricken mother's soul!
All swims before her eyes, flashes with black, she catches the main
      words only,
Sentences broken, *gunshot wound in the breast, cavalry skirmish,
      taken to hospital,*
At present low, but will soon be better.

Ah now the single figure to me,
Amid all teeming and wealthy Ohio with all its cities and farms,
Sickly white in the face and dull in the head, very faint,
By the jamb of a door leans.

Grieve not so, dear mother, (the just-grown daughter speaks through
      her sobs,

The little sisters huddle around speechless and dismay'd,)
See, dearest mother, the letter says Pete will soon be better.

Alas poor boy, he will never be better, (nor may-be needs to be
        better, that brave and simple soul,)
While they stand at home at the door he is dead already,
The only son is dead.

But the mother needs to be better,
She with thin form presently drest in black,
By day her meals untouch'd, then at night fitfully sleeping, often
        waking,
In the midnight waking, weeping, longing with one deep longing,
O that she might withdraw unnoticed, silent from life escape and
        withdraw,
To follow, to seek, to be with her dear dead son.

VIGIL STRANGE I KEPT ON THE FIELD ONE NIGHT.

Vigil strange I kept on the field one night;
  When you my son and my comrade dropt at my side that day,
  One look I but gave which your dear eyes return'd with a look I shall
      never forget,
  One touch of your hand to mine O boy, reach'd up as you lay on the
      ground,
  Then onward I sped in the battle, the even-contested battle,
  Till late in the night reliev'd to the place at last again I made my
      way,
  Found you in death so cold dear comrade, found your body son of
      responding kisses, (never again on earth responding,)
  Bared your face in the starlight, curious the scene, cool blew the
      moderate night-wind,
  Long there and then in vigil I stood, dimly around me the
      battle-field spreading,
  Vigil wondrous and vigil sweet there in the fragrant silent night,
  But not a tear fell, not even a long-drawn sigh, long, long I gazed,
  Then on the earth partially reclining sat by your side leaning my
      chin in my hands,
  Passing sweet hours, immortal and mystic hours with you dearest
      comrade—not a tear, not a word,
  Vigil of silence, love and death, vigil for you my son and my
      soldier,
  As onward silently stars aloft, eastward new ones upward stole,
  Vigil final for you brave boy, (I could not save you, swift was your
      death,
  I faithfully loved you and cared for you living, I think we shall
      surely meet again,)
  Till at latest lingering of the night, indeed just as the dawn
      appear'd,
  My comrade I wrapt in his blanket, envelop'd well his form,
  Folded the blanket well, tucking it carefully over head and carefully
      under feet,
  And there and then and bathed by the rising sun, my son in his grave,
      in his rude-dug grave I deposited,
  Ending my vigil strange with that, vigil of night and battle-field
      dim,
  Vigil for boy of responding kisses, (never again on earth
      responding,)

Vigil for comrade swiftly slain, vigil I never forget, how as day
     brighten'd,
I rose from the chill ground and folded my soldier well in his
     blanket,
And buried him where he fell.

A MARCH IN THE RANKS HARD-PREST, AND THE ROAD UNKNOWN.

A march in the ranks hard-prest, and the road unknown,
  A route through a heavy wood with muffled steps in the darkness,
  Our army foil'd with loss severe, and the sullen remnant retreating,
  Till after midnight glimmer upon us the lights of a dim-lighted
      building,
  We come to an open space in the woods, and halt by the dim-lighted
      building,
  'Tis a large old church at the crossing roads, now an impromptu
      hospital,
  Entering but for a minute I see a sight beyond all the pictures and
      poems ever made,
  Shadows of deepest, deepest black, just lit by moving candles and
      lamps,
  And by one great pitchy torch stationary with wild red flame and
      clouds of smoke,
  By these, crowds, groups of forms vaguely I see on the floor, some in
      the pews laid down,
  At my feet more distinctly a soldier, a mere lad, in danger of
      bleeding to death, (he is shot in the abdomen,)
  I staunch the blood temporarily, (the youngster's face is white as a
      lily,)
  Then before I depart I sweep my eyes o'er the scene fain to absorb it
      all,
  Faces, varieties, postures beyond description, most in obscurity,
      some of them dead,
  Surgeons operating, attendants holding lights, the smell of ether,
      the odor of blood,
  The crowd, O the crowd of the bloody forms, the yard outside also
      fill'd,
  Some on the bare ground, some on planks or stretchers, some in the
      death-spasm sweating,
  An occasional scream or cry, the doctor's shouted orders or calls,
  The glisten of the little steel instruments catching the glint of the
      torches,
  These I resume as I chant, I see again the forms, I smell the odor,
  Then hear outside the orders given, *Fall in, my men, fall in;*
  But first I bend to the dying lad, his eyes open, a half-smile gives
      he me,

Then the eyes close, calmly close, and I speed forth to the darkness,
Resuming, marching, ever in darkness marching, on in the ranks,
The unknown road still marching.

A SIGHT IN CAMP IN THE DAYBREAK GRAY AND DIM.

A sight in camp in the daybreak gray and dim,
  As from my tent I emerge so early sleepless,
  As slow I walk in the cool fresh air the path near by the hospital
      tent,
  Three forms I see on stretchers lying, brought out there untended
      lying,
  Over each the blanket spread, ample brownish woollen blanket,
  Gray and heavy blanket, folding, covering all.

  Curious I halt and silent stand,
  Then with light fingers I from the face of the nearest the first just
      lift the blanket;
  Who are you elderly man so gaunt and grim, with well-gray'd hair, and
      flesh all sunken about the eyes?
  Who are you my dear comrade?

  Then to the second I step—and who are you my child and darling?
  Who are you sweet boy with cheeks yet blooming?

  Then to the third—a face nor child nor old, very calm, as of
      beautiful yellow-white ivory;
  Young man I think I know you—I think this face is the face of the
      Christ himself,
  Dead and divine and brother of all, and here again he lies.

AS TOILSOME I WANDER'D VIRGINIA'S WOODS.

As toilsome I wander'd Virginia's woods,
  To the music of rustling leaves kick'd by my feet, (for 'twas autumn,)
  I mark'd at the foot of a tree the grave of a soldier;
  Mortally wounded he and buried on the retreat, (easily all could I
      understand,)
  The halt of a mid-day hour, when up! no time to lose-yet this sign
      left,
  On a tablet scrawl'd and nail'd on the tree by the grave,
  Bold, cautious, true, and my loving comrade.

Long, long I muse, then on my way go wandering,
Many a changeful season to follow, and many a scene of life,
Yet at times through changeful season and scene, abrupt, alone, or in
      the crowded street,
Comes before me the unknown soldier's grave, comes the inscription
      rude in Virginia's woods,

  Bold, cautious, true, and my loving comrade.

NOT THE PILOT.

Not the pilot has charged himself to bring his ship into port,
  though beaten back and many times baffled;
  Not the pathfinder penetrating inland weary and long,
  By deserts parch'd, snows chill'd, rivers wet, perseveres till he
      reaches his destination,
  More than I have charged myself, heeded or unheeded, to compose a
      march for these States,
  For a battle-call, rousing to arms if need be, years, centuries
      hence.

YEAR THAT TREMBLED AND REEL'D BENEATH ME.

Year that trembled and reel'd beneath me!
Your summer wind was warm enough, yet the air I breathed froze me,
  A thick gloom fell through the sunshine and darken'd me,
  Must I change my triumphant songs? said I to myself,
  Must I indeed learn to chant the cold dirges of the baffled?
  And sullen hymns of defeat?

THE WOUND-DRESSER.

1

An old man bending I come among new faces,
  Years looking backward resuming in answer to children,
  Come tell us old man, as from young men and maidens that love me,
  (Arous'd and angry, I'd thought to beat the alarum, and urge
        relentless war,
  But soon my fingers fail'd me, my face droop'd and I resign'd myself,
  To sit by the wounded and soothe them, or silently watch the dead;)
  Years hence of these scenes, of these furious passions, these
        chances,
  Of unsurpass'd heroes, (was one side so brave? the other was equally
        brave;)
  Now be witness again, paint the mightiest armies of earth,
  Of those armies so rapid so wondrous what saw you to tell us?
  What stays with you latest and deepest? of curious panics,
  Of hard-fought engagements or sieges tremendous what deepest
        remains?

2

      O maidens and young men I love and that love me,
  What you ask of my days those the strangest and sudden your talking
        recalls,
  Soldier alert I arrive after a long march cover'd with sweat and
        dust,
  In the nick of time I come, plunge in the fight, loudly shout in the
        rush of successful charge,
  Enter the captur'd works—yet lo, like a swift-running river they
        fade,
  Pass and are gone they fade—I dwell not on soldiers' perils or
        soldiers' joys,
  (Both I remember well—many the hardships, few the joys, yet I was
        content.)

  But in silence, in dreams' projections,
  While the world of gain and appearance and mirth goes on,
  So soon what is over forgotten, and waves wash the imprints off the
        sand,
  With hinged knees returning I enter the doors, (while for you up

there,
Whoever you are, follow without noise and be of strong heart.)

Bearing the bandages, water and sponge,
Straight and swift to my wounded I go,
Where they lie on the ground after the battle brought in,
Where their priceless blood reddens the grass the ground,
Or to the rows of the hospital tent, or under the roof'd hospital,
To the long rows of cots up and down each side I return,
To each and all one after another I drawn near, not one do I miss,
An attendant follows holding a tray, he carries a refuse pail,
Soon to be fill'd with clotted rags and blood, emptied, and fill'd
    again.

I onward go, I stop,
With hinged knees and steady hand to dress wounds,
I am firm with each, the pangs are sharp yet unavoidable,
One turns to me his appealing eyes-poor boy! I never knew you,
Yet I think I could not refuse this moment to die for you, if that
    would save you.

3

On, on I go, (open doors of time! open hospital doors!)
  The crush'd head I dress, (poor crazed hand tear not the bandage
    away,)
  The neck of the cavalry-man with the bullet through and through I
    examine,
  Hard the breathing rattles, quite glazed already the eye, yet life
    struggles hard,
  (Come sweet death! be persuaded O beautiful death!
  In mercy come quickly.)

From the stump of the arm, the amputated hand,
  I undo the clotted lint, remove the slough, wash off the matter and
    blood,
  Back on his pillow the soldier bends with curv'd neck and
    side-falling head,
  His eyes are closed, his face is pale, he dares not look on the
    bloody stump,
  And has not yet look'd on it.

I dress a wound in the side, deep, deep,

But a day or two more, for see the frame all wasted and sinking,
And the yellow-blue countenance see.

I dress the perforated shoulder, the foot with the bullet-wound,
Cleanse the one with a gnawing and putrid gangrene, so sickening, so
    offensive,
While the attendant stands behind aside me holding the tray and pail.

I am faithful, I do not give out,
The fractur'd thigh, the knee, the wound in the abdomen,
These and more I dress with impassive hand, (yet deep in my breast a
    fire, a burning flame.)

4

Thus in silence in dreams' projections,
  Returning, resuming, I thread my way through the hospitals,
  The hurt and wounded I pacify with soothing hand,
  I sit by the restless all the dark night, some are so young,
  Some suffer so much, I recall the experience sweet and sad,
  (Many a soldier's loving arms about this neck have cross'd and
    rested,
  Many a soldier's kiss dwells on these bearded lips.)

LONG, TOO LONG AMERICA.

Long, too long America,
  Traveling roads all even and peaceful you learn'd from joys and
      prosperity only,
  But now, ah now, to learn from crises of anguish, advancing,
      grappling with direst fate and recoiling not,
  And now to conceive and show to the world what your children en-masse
      really are,
  (For who except myself has yet conceiv'd what your children en-
    masse really are?)

GIVE ME THE SPLENDID SILENT SUN.

1

Give me the splendid silent sun with all his beams full-dazzling,
Give me juicy autumnal fruit ripe and red from the orchard,
Give me a field where the unmow'd grass grows,
Give me an arbor, give me the trellis'd grape,
Give me fresh corn and wheat, give me serene-moving animals teaching
content,
Give me nights perfectly quiet as on high plateaus west of the
Mississippi, and I looking up at the stars,
Give me odorous at sunrise a garden of beautiful flowers where I can
walk undisturb'd,
Give me for marriage a sweet-breath'd woman of whom I should never
tire,
Give me a perfect child, give me away aside from the noise of the
world a rural domestic life,
Give me to warble spontaneous songs recluse by myself, for my own
ears only,
Give me solitude, give me Nature, give me again O Nature your primal
sanities!

These demanding to have them, (tired with ceaseless excitement, and
rack'd by the war-strife,)
These to procure incessantly asking, rising in cries from my heart,
While yet incessantly asking still I adhere to my city,
Day upon day and year upon year O city, walking your streets,
Where you hold me enchain'd a certain time refusing to give me up,
Yet giving to make me glutted, enrich'd of soul, you give me forever
faces;
(O I see what I sought to escape, confronting, reversing my cries,
I see my own soul trampling down what it ask'd for.)

2

Keep your splendid silent sun,
Keep your woods O Nature, and the quiet places by the woods,
Keep your fields of clover and timothy, and your corn-fields and
orchards,
Keep the blossoming buckwheat fields where the Ninth-month bees hum;

Give me faces and streets—give me these phantoms incessant and
    endless along the trottoirs!
Give me interminable eyes—give me women—give me comrades and
    lovers by the thousand!
Let me see new ones every day—let me hold new ones by the hand every
    day!
Give me such shows—give me the streets of Manhattan!
Give me Broadway, with the soldiers marching—give me the sound of
    the trumpets and drums!
(The soldiers in companies or regiments—some starting away, flush'd
    and reckless,
Some, their time up, returning with thinn'd ranks, young, yet very
    old, worn, marching, noticing nothing;)
Give me the shores and wharves heavy-fringed with black ships!
O such for me! O an intense life, full to repletion and varied!
The life of the theatre, bar-room, huge hotel, for me!
The saloon of the steamer! the crowded excursion for me! the
    torchlight procession!
The dense brigade bound for the war, with high piled military wagons
    following;
People, endless, streaming, with strong voices, passions, pageants,
Manhattan streets with their powerful throbs, with beating drums as
    now,
The endless and noisy chorus, the rustle and clank of muskets, (even
    the sight of the wounded,)
Manhattan crowds, with their turbulent musical chorus!
Manhattan faces and eyes forever for me.

DIRGE FOR TWO VETERANS.

The last sunbeam
  Lightly falls from the finish'd Sabbath,
  On the pavement here, and there beyond it is looking,
    Down a new-made double grave.

  Lo, the moon ascending,
Up from the east the silvery round moon,
Beautiful over the house-tops, ghastly, phantom moon,
    Immense and silent moon.

  I see a sad procession,
And I hear the sound of coming full-key'd bugles,
All the channels of the city streets they're flooding,
    As with voices and with tears.

  I hear the great drums pounding,
And the small drums steady whirring,
And every blow of the great convulsive drums,
    Strikes me through and through.

  For the son is brought with the father,
(In the foremost ranks of the fierce assault they fell,
Two veterans son and father dropt together,
    And the double grave awaits them.)

  Now nearer blow the bugles,
And the drums strike more convulsive,
And the daylight o'er the pavement quite has faded,
    And the strong dead-march enwraps me.

  In the eastern sky up-buoying,
The sorrowful vast phantom moves illumin'd,
('Tis some mother's large transparent face,
    In heaven brighter growing.)

  O strong dead-march you please me!
O moon immense with your silvery face you soothe me!
O my soldiers twain! O my veterans passing to burial!
    What I have I also give you.

The moon gives you light,
And the bugles and the drums give you music,
And my heart, O my soldiers, my veterans,
My heart gives you love.

OVER THE CARNAGE ROSE PROPHETIC A VOICE.

Over the carnage rose prophetic a voice,
  Be not dishearten'd, affection shall solve the problems of freedom
    yet,
  Those who love each other shall become invincible,
  They shall yet make Columbia victorious.

Sons of the Mother of All, you shall yet be victorious,
  You shall yet laugh to scorn the attacks of all the remainder of the
    earth.

No danger shall balk Columbia's lovers,
  If need be a thousand shall sternly immolate themselves for one.
  One from Massachusetts shall be a Missourian's comrade,
  From Maine and from hot Carolina, and another an Oregonese, shall be
    friends triune,
  More precious to each other than all the riches of the earth.

To Michigan, Florida perfumes shall tenderly come,
  Not the perfumes of flowers, but sweeter, and wafted beyond death.

It shall be customary in the houses and streets to see manly
    affection,
  The most dauntless and rude shall touch face to face lightly,
  The dependence of Liberty shall be lovers,
  The continuance of equality shall be comrades.

These shall tie you and band you stronger than hoops of iron,
  I, ecstatic, O partners! O lands! with the love of lovers tie you.

(Were you looking to be held together by lawyers?
  Or by an agreement on a paper? or by arms?
  Nay, nor the world, nor any living thing, will so cohere.)

I SAW OLD GENERAL AT BAY.

I saw old General at bay,
  (Old as he was, his gray eyes yet shone out in battle like stars,)
  His small force was now completely hemm'd in, in his works,
  He call'd for volunteers to run the enemy's lines, a desperate
      emergency,
  I saw a hundred and more step forth from the ranks, but two or three
      were selected,
  I saw them receive their orders aside, they listen'd with care, the
      adjutant was very grave,
  I saw them depart with cheerfulness, freely risking their lives.

THE ARTILLERYMAN'S VISION.

While my wife at my side lies slumbering, and the wars are over long,
  And my head on the pillow rests at home, and the vacant midnight
      passes,
  And through the stillness, through the dark, I hear, just hear, the
      breath of my infant,
There in the room as I wake from sleep this vision presses upon me;
The engagement opens there and then in fantasy unreal,
The skirmishers begin, they crawl cautiously ahead, I hear the
      irregular snap! snap!
I hear the sounds of the different missiles, the short *t-h-t!*
      t-h-t! of the rifle-balls,
I see the shells exploding leaving small white clouds, I hear the
      great shells shrieking as they pass,
The grape like the hum and whirr of wind through the trees
      (tumultuous now the contest rages,)
All the scenes at the batteries rise in detail before me again,
The crashing and smoking, the pride of the men in their pieces,
The chief-gunner ranges and sights his piece and selects a fuse of
      the right time,
After firing I see him lean aside and look eagerly off to note the
      effect;
Elsewhere I hear the cry of a regiment charging, (the young colonel
      leads himself this time with brandish'd sword,)
I see the gaps cut by the enemy's volleys, (quickly fill'd up, no
      delay,)
I breathe the suffocating smoke, then the flat clouds hover low
      concealing all;
Now a strange lull for a few seconds, not a shot fired on either
      side,
Then resumed the chaos louder than ever, with eager calls and orders
      of officers,
While from some distant part of the field the wind wafts to my ears a
      shout of applause, (some special success,)
And ever the sound of the cannon far or near, (rousing even in dreams
      a devilish exultation and all the old mad joy in the depths
      of my soul,)
And ever the hastening of infantry shifting positions, batteries,
      cavalry, moving hither and thither,
(The falling, dying, I heed not, the wounded dripping and red I heed

not, some to the rear are hobbling,)
Grime, heat, rush, aide-de-camps galloping by or on a full run,
With the patter of small arms, the warning *s-s-t* of the rifles,
    (these in my vision I hear or see,)
And bombs bursting in air, and at night the vari-color'd rockets.

ETHIOPIA SALUTING THE COLOURS.

Who are you dusky woman, so ancient hardly human,
  With your woolly-white and turban'd head, and bare bony feet
  Why rising by the roadside here, do you the colours greet?

('Tis while our army lines Carolina's sands and pines,
Forth from thy hovel door thou Ethiopia com'st to me,
As under doughty Sherman I march toward the sea.)

Me master years a hundred since from my parents sunder'd,
A little child, they caught me as the savage beast is caught,
Then hither me across the sea the cruel slaver brought.

No further does she say, but lingering all the day,
Her high-borne turban'd head she wags, and rolls her darkling eye,
And courtesies to the regiments, the guidons moving by.

What is it fateful woman, so blear, hardly human?
Why wag your head with turban bound, yellow, red and green?
Are the things so strange and marvellous you see or have seen?

NOT YOUTH PERTAINS TO ME.

Not youth pertains to me,
  Nor delicatesse, I cannot beguile the time with talk,
  Awkward in the parlor, neither a dancer nor elegant,
  In the learn'd coterie sitting constrain'd and still, for learning
       inures not to me,
  Beauty, knowledge, inure not to me-yet there are two or three things
       inure to me,
  I have nourish'd the wounded and sooth'd many a dying soldier,
  And at intervals waiting or in the midst of camp,
  Composed these songs.

RACE OF VETERANS.

Race of veterans—race of victors!
  Race of the soil, ready for conflict—race of the conquering march;
  (No more credulity's race, abiding-temper'd race,)
  Race henceforth owning no law but the law of itself,
            Race of passion and the storm.

WORLD TAKE GOOD NOTICE.

World take good notice, silver stars fading,
  Milky hue ript, weft of white detaching,
  Coals thirty-eight, baleful and burning,
  Scarlet, significant, hands off warning,
  Now and henceforth flaunt from these shores

O TAN-FACED PRAIRIE-BOY.

O tan-faced prairie-boy,
  Before you came to camp came many a welcome gift,
  Praises and presents came and nourishing food, till at last among the
      recruits,
  You came, taciturn, with nothing to give-we but look'd on each other,
  When lo; more than all the gifts of the world you gave me.

LOOK DOWN FAIR MOON.

Look down fair moon and bathe this scene,
  Pour softly down night's nimbus floods on faces ghastly, swollen,
      purple,
  On the dead on their backs with arms toss'd wide,
  Pour down your unstinted nimbus sacred moon.

RECONCILIATION.

Word over all, beautiful as the sky,
   Beautiful that war and all its deeds of carnage must in time be
       utterly lost,
   That the hands of the sisters Death and Night incessantly softly wash
       again, and ever again, this soil'd world;
   For my enemy is dead, a man divine as myself is dead,
   I look where he lies white-faced and still in the coffin-I draw near,
   Bend down and touch lightly with my lips the white face in the
       coffin.

HOW SOLEMN AS ONE BY ONE.

(Washington City, 1865.)

How solemn as one by one,
  As the ranks returning worn and sweaty, as the men file by where I
      stand,
  As the faces the masks appear, as I glance at the faces studying the
      masks,
  (As I glance upward out of this page studying you, dear friend,
      whoever you are,)
  How solemn the thought of my whispering soul to each in the ranks,
      and to you,
  I see behind each mask that wonder a kindred soul,
  O the bullet could never kill what you really are, dear friend,
  Nor the bayonet stab what you really are;
  The soul! yourself I see, great as any, good as the best,
  Waiting secure and content, which the bullet could never kill,
  Nor the bayonet stab O friend.

AS I LAY WITH MY HEAD IN YOUR LAP CAMERADO.

As I lay with my head in your lap camerado,
  The confession I made I resume, what I said to you and the open air I
    resume,
  I know I am restless and make others so,
  I know my words are weapons full of danger, full of death,
  For I confront peace, security, and all the settled laws, to unsettle
    them,
  I am more resolute because all have denied me than I could ever have
    been had all accepted me,
  I heed not and have never heeded either experience, cautions,
    majorities, nor ridicule,
  And the threat of what is call'd hell is little or nothing to me;
  And the lure of what is call'd heaven is little or nothing to me;
  Dear camerado! I confess I have urged you onward with me, and still
    urge you, without the least idea what is our destination,
  Or whether we shall be victorious, or utterly quell'd and defeated.

DELICATE CLUSTER.

Delicate cluster! flag of teeming life!
  Covering all my lands-all my seashores lining!
  Flag of death! (how I watch'd you through the smoke of battle
      pressing!
  How I heard you flap and rustle, cloth defiant!)
  Flag cerulean-sunny flag, with the orbs of night dappled!
  Ah my silvery beauty-ah my woolly white and crimson!
  Ah to sing the song of you, my matron mighty!
  My sacred one, my mother.

TO A CERTAIN CIVILIAN.

Did you ask dulcet rhymes from me?
　Did you seek the civilian's peaceful and languishing rhymes?
　Did you find what I sang erewhile so hard to follow?
　Why I was not singing erewhile for you to follow, to understand—nor
　　　am I now;
　(I have been born of the same as the war was born,
　The drum-corps' rattle is ever to me sweet music, I love well the
　　　martial dirge,
　With slow wail and convulsive throb leading the officer's funeral;)
　What to such as you anyhow such a poet as I? therefore leave my
　　　works,
　And go lull yourself with what you can understand, and with
　　　piano-tunes,
　For I lull nobody, and you will never understand me.

LO, VICTRESS ON THE PEAKS.

Lo, Victress on the peaks,
  Where thou with mighty brow regarding the world,
  (The world O Libertad, that vainly conspired against thee,)
  Out of its countless beleaguering toils, after thwarting them all,
  Dominant, with the dazzling sun around thee,
  Flauntest now unharm'd in immortal soundness and bloom—lo, in
      these
        hours supreme,
  No poem proud, I chanting bring to thee, nor mastery's rapturous
      verse,
  But a cluster containing night's darkness and blood-dripping wounds,
               And psalms of the dead.

SPIRIT WHOSE WORK IS DONE.

(Washington City, 1865.)

Spirit whose work is done—spirit of dreadful hours!
  Ere departing fade from my eyes your forests of bayonets;
  Spirit of gloomiest fears and doubts, (yet onward ever unfaltering
      pressing),
  Spirit of many a solemn day and many a savage scene—electric spirit,
  That with muttering voice through the war now closed, like a tireless
      phantom flitted,
  Rousing the land with breath of flame, while you beat and beat the
      drum,
  Now as the sound of the drum, hollow and harsh to the last,
      reverberates round me,
  As your ranks, your immortal ranks, return, return from the battles,
  As the muskets of the young men yet lean over their shoulders,
  As I look on the bayonets bristling over their shoulders,
  As those slanted bayonets, whole forests of them appearing in the
      distance, approach and pass on, returning homeward,
  Moving with steady motion, swaying to and fro to the right and left,
  Evenly lightly rising and falling while the steps keep time;
  Spirit of hours I knew, all hectic red one day, but pale as death
      next day,
  Touch my mouth ere you depart, press my lips close,
  Leave me your pulses of rage—bequeath them to me—fill me with
      currents convulsive,
  Let them scorch and blister out of my chants when you are gone,
  Let them identify you to the future in these songs.

ADIEU TO A SOLDIER.

Adieu O soldier,
  You of the rude campaigning, (which we shared,)
  The rapid march, the life of the camp,
  The hot contention of opposing fronts, the long manoeuvre,
  Bed battles with their slaughter, the stimulus, the strong, terrific
      game,
  Spell of all brave and manly hearts, the trains of time through you
      and like of you all fill'd,
  With war and war's expression.

Adieu dear comrade,
  Your mission is fulfill'd—but I, more warlike,
  Myself and this contentious soul of mine,
  Still on our own campaigning bound,
  Through untried roads with ambushes opponents lined,
  Through many a sharp defeat and many a crisis, often baffled,
  Here marching, ever marching on, a war fight out—aye here,
  To fiercer, weightier battles give expression.

TURN O LIBERTAD.

Turn O Libertad, for the war is over,
  From it and all henceforth expanding, doubting no more, resolute,
      sweeping the world,
  Turn from lands retrospective recording proofs of the past,
  From the singers that sing the trailing glories of the past,
  From the chants of the feudal world, the triumphs of kings, slavery,
      caste,
  Turn to the world, the triumphs reserv'd and to come—give up that
      backward world,
  Leave to the singers of hitherto, give them the trailing past,
  But what remains remains for singers for you—wars to come are for
      you,
  (Lo, how the wars of the past have duly inured to you, and the wars
      of the present also inure;)
  Then turn, and be not alarm'd O Libertad—turn your undying face,
  To where the future, greater than all the past,
  Is swiftly, surely preparing for you.

TO THE LEAVEN'D SOIL THEY TROD.

To the leaven'd soil they trod calling I sing for the last,
  (Forth from my tent emerging for good, loosing, untying the
        tent-ropes,)
  In the freshness the forenoon air, in the far-stretching circuits and
        vistas again to peace restored,
  To the fiery fields emanative and the endless vistas beyond, to the
        South and the North,
  To the leaven'd soil of the general Western world to attest my songs,
  To the Alleghanian hills and the tireless Mississippi,
  To the rocks I calling sing, and all the trees in the woods,
  To the plains of the poems of heroes, to the prairies spreading wide,
  To the far-off sea and the unseen winds, and the sane impalpable air;
  And responding they answer all, (but not in words,)
  The average earth, the witness of war and peace, acknowledges mutely,
  The prairie draws me close, as the father to bosom broad the son,
  The Northern ice and rain that began me nourish me to the end,
  But the hot sun of the South is to fully ripen my songs.